Open Plan

Open Plan
Graham Fulton

Published 2011 by
Smokestack Books
PO Box 408, Middlesbrough TS5 6WA
e-mail : info@smokestack-books.co.uk
www.smokestack-books.co.uk

Open Plan
Graham Fulton
Copyright 2011, Graham Fulton, all rights reserved
Cover photograph: Graham Fulton

Printed by
EPW Print & Design Ltd

ISBN 978-0-9564175-6-5
Smokestack Books gratefully
acknowledges the support of
Arts Council England

Smokestack Books is
represented by Inpress Ltd
www.inpressbooks.co.uk

Some of these poems have been published before in
Northwords Now, Pennine Ink and *poetrymonthly.com*

for Alan McCready, a weesaint

Contents

- 11 dark matter
- 12 log on
- 13 food chain
- 14 multi tasking
- 15 private sector
- 16 down size
- 17 bondage game
- 18 people skills
- 19 brain wave
- 20 remote control
- 21 royal court
- 22 egg man
- 23 alien nation
- 24 shock treatment
- 25 paperless office
- 26 special K
- 27 suspect device
- 28 time management
- 29 new mail
- 30 bad timing
- 31 team meeting
- 32 out standing
- 33 learning curve
- 34 satellite pish
- 35 smoke ring
- 36 drink problem
- 37 reliable information
- 38 door crime
- 39 cloud cuckoo
- 40 war correspondent
- 41 transporter malfunction
- 42 rocket science
- 43 tea time
- 44 fertile ground

45 minority report
46 defective units
47 donkey sanctuary
48 lost cause
49 laptop dancer
50 cabin fever
51 bad taste
52 paper jam
53 and relax
54 press gang
55 block buster
56 unnatural habitat
57 ladies man
58 hot desking
59 baby food
60 definite article
61 resigner bubble
62 recycle bin
63 set menu
64 new start
65 bad magnet
66 glass ceiling
67 inappropriate use
68 love story
69 vanishing point
70 log off
72 nostra bamus

dark matter

the lights are asleep
   and
the switched off office
    is tingling
  with all
the passwords
 waiting to be changed
and the toilets
   waiting to be flushed
and the numbers
     waiting to be crunched
and the clocks
      waiting to be watched
and the systems
    waiting to be crashed
and the bucks
   waiting to be passed
              and
a space
      waiting to be filled
and the holes
      waiting
to be black

log on

Tony Loony
    turns himself
on
  and feeds in
      his name
     tells me to say
My Precious
     in the voice of Gollum
and *Hello my name is John Merrick*
    in the voice of John Merrick
and *The Lord Is My Shepherd*
in the voice of Edward Woodward
     as he burns to death
directly
into a microphone
      before playing it
down the line to an ex employee
       who hasn't been forgotten
long enough
      to even
become a
      memory

food chain

the Serengeti
  open plan office
is sliced into
     hard little pods
which are diced
        into hard little
work stations
          with all new desks
and all old chairs
          on which we perch
in a theoretically
        ergonomically friendly way
with our backs exposed
     which goes against our need
for defensible space
     in case a lion or wolf decides
to hunt us for lunch with only
   our paper clips and protractors and
correction fluid for weapons

multi tasking

John the fount of knowledge
        enters the pod
to insert some brand
        spanking software
crucial to the lubrication
        of our shite of
the art
    technology
                        pauses
        to brighten our day
with one handed juggling
        of two satsumas
and
  tells a joke
        the length of
Crime and Punishment
        only not as funny
as we double click
        our mice
        and remember
to laugh

private sector

there are 3 cubicles
    in the Gents toilet
and sometimes you go in
      to get away
and somebody's already in one
        because you can see his feet
and he's keeping really quiet
          and hoping you'll quickly leave
and
sometimes
it's you that's in the cubicle
and somebody comes in
so you keep really quiet
      or do
a courtesy flush
to let them know you're there
     and on particularly
dramatic occasions
        all 3 cubicles are occupied
and you're all
         keeping really quiet
because no-one
          wants to be
the first to crack

down size

Alan's second name
 is McCready
   as in Freddy
 but everyone
     calls him McCready
as in Seedy
     despite being told
over
   and over
again
by Alan
who happens to have
     a rare genetic condition
         which has left him
             smaller than normal
and
with big shoulders
   to carry both chips
so he's decided
   to christen himself a himp
which is a cross between
     a hobbit and a chimp
which seems fair enough

bondage game

Steven rings
  a victim
and says
    You've got to
come and see
        This
and
you hurry
  expectantly
to his pod
     and he lifts
a piece of paper
       on his desk
to reveal another piece
     with the word
       THIS
on it
          or
he pings elastic bands
      at you or stretches
several bands
     around his head
to turn himself
      grotesque
at times
        of supreme tedium

people skills

Bob the big boned receptionist
      stops in the middle
of listening
    to a public member
  and seamlessly proceeds
to lift his leg
  and loudly fart
      and proudly proclaim *Good Arse!*
  in one expertly fluid movement
before continuing
    to listen
to the public member
      who seamlessly proceeds
to lift
  his pen
and file a perfectly
         inevitable complaint
as if nothing
        had really
happened

brain wave

the Huge Head
  in his wisdom
decides that
  what is currently C
    must quickly become B
      which will make
       thinking
much safer
     for himself
in the brave new world
   of gods and monsters
       which
turns out to be
    a heap
of keech
            and what
used to be C
   and is now B
     must return
     to being C
a.s.a.p.
       before it's
too late

remote control

giving someone
    a name
without their knowledge
  creates a sense
of power
       so
    one officer
       is called *Mini Pip*
    because he looks
like a pipistrel bat
  or *Nostrildamus*
because he has
    lots of hair
coming out of his nose
    and finally
       The Mother Pip
  because
we can feel him
    hoovering up
      our will to live
  like a malevolent
alien parasite

royal court

Prince John
   blows raspberries
and laughs like
      a cappuccino machine
and blethers never
      endingly on
and on
        about Beethoven
and the stock market
        and having your teeth
pulled out when
    you get married
as everybody else
   in the pod
pays no attention
and announces
   that he's going
home early to watch
   Big Brother
because *There's*
    so much more
to life than THIS

egg man

King Man comes up
   and asks me
         if I think Kennedy
was shot by Andy Warhol
on the grassy knoll
       and if it's really
Paul McCartney
     walking across
         the zebra crossing
with a cigarette in his right hand
 and if Neil Armstrong
said *That's one small step*
   for Man on
a plastic moon
in Texas
and was Martin Luther Kong
  a white man
     and did the Sixties
really exist

alien nation

Tony Loony
    takes a
well-earned break
from
    creating
committee deadline reports
  and lifts the lid
of the scanner
     slaps his face
down on the glass
and happily
commences
     to scan
it
  while
shoogling
   his head about
to make him look
    like a Martian
from *The Outer Limits*

shock treatment

well-dressed
        Mick the Stick
who is searching
         for better things
concentrates so hard
        he never knows
John the fount of knowledge
      has walked up behind him
and leaps out his skin
       every single time
with
   his heart hammering
    and his face gone red
even when John makes
       madly exaggerated
   stamping noises
that everyone else
  in the whole building
can hear

paperless office

Steven buys
        a tabloid each morning
            with pages of ladies
wearing smiles
        and knickers
        and not much else
which everyone turns
        their noses up at
because it's degrading
to women
        except
when Steven's
        out to lunch
and we're
        fighting to get
the first shot

special K

Katie the existential typist
    who may be thirty
or fifty if I took
    the time to find out
beetles between
        the ceiling-high shelves
           creaking beneath
the weight of
    the Kafkaesque files
and whispers
        conspiratorially
    to herself as she keeps
        her eyes on her feet
with a brown sandal
        on the left and
           a black leather
on the right

suspect device

every button on
        the 21st Century
all-singing all-dancing
multi function device
        that faxes
          scans
        folds and staples
whether you want
    it to or not
  makes a high pitched
bleeping noise that
    machetes into
  your bleeping brain
especially when three
    are bleeping at bleeping once
and you're starting to
        hear them in
your bleeping sleep

time management

Alan the endangered himp
      flamboyantly squiggles
on one of my yellow stickies
then stands back
  to admire
what looks like
    a saggy breast
in profile
      with
a belly below
and a neck
above
      and
        we
slowly discuss
       the well
of the subconscious
     which uses up
a few more minutes at
    the ratepayers' expense

new mail

the communication
      of information
has never been easier
      because of massive
megabyte advances
        such as the internet
which we use to make
    the lives of
the taxpayers better
   by sending pictures
to each other
of genuine
  foreign products
such as *Coolpis* fruitjuice
     and *Big Nuts* chocolate
and *My Fannie* kitchen roll
       and *BumBum* banana gum
and *Fart* juice and *Cock* soup
     and *Homo* soap and
we giggle like girls
till it's time for tea

bad timing

Dave the Rave
   worships a girl
                    from a distant pod
   called *The Goddess*
but is off for a pish
    when she steps into ours
for the one
      and only
           time
  in need of manly assistance
and when
   he strolls back
we give him the bad news
             and he lies
  down on the carpet
      and curls
into a foetal position
        and pretends
to cry
    just as
        the Huge Head
happens to walk by

team meeting

instead of listening intently
                to lots of stuff
    about *Changes*
and *Performance*
  and *Deadlines*
  and *Outcomes*
              everyone
         sits
    and thinks about *Sex*
          or *Soap*
       or *Golf* or
      Sex or *Food* or
    Beer or
doodles
    mutated humans with
       large misshapen heads
and no genitals
   in a brave attempt
to keep awake
          which doesn't
always succeed

out standing

Alan the endangered himp
   is reading a book
about the Vietnam War
     and remorselessly
bombs the conversation
        with coolness like
Incoming
     and *DMZ*
and *Agent Orange*
        and *FNG*
and
           waxes nostalgic
about the smell
     of napalm
in the morning
     and how he can't
wait
   to rotate
back
   to The World
as he sticks his card
       in the flexi machine

learning curve

King Man comes up
        and asks me
 who Charles Manson is
and who Sharon Tate is
        and asks me why
                he did
                        It
        and what movies
      Ronan Peloonski made
and who else he killed
        and if he's still alive
   or did he die at Waco
or did he die at Columbine
and what does chaos theory mean
                and is it possible
to get in touch
with him by email
which it probably is

satellite pish

Prince John
  spins on his chair
   and announces that
he's got a twitch in his left eye
  undoubtedly brought on
by overwork
   or stress
    or the fact
that he sits up
till five in the morning
surfing the Sky channels
   and we all
dutifully troop up
   and take it in turns
    to gaze at his face
and completely agree
    it's the best twitch
     we've ever seen
which makes his day

smoke ring

a happy few addicts
    flock outside
the main doors
        in the wind and
    the snow and
       the rain
to exchange willpower tales
      and harvest
      the contents of their lungs
        and
            suck
    whatever it is
   they're hoping
      to find
into their brains
       and out again
with a desperate useless
joy

drink problem

wee Senga can't say
Jack Daniels
        so her pals
keep on and on
    until she
finally gives in
        and says
Jack Janiels
and *Dack Ganiels*
    and *Jock Spaniels*
and *Jack Janiels* and
    Jack Janiels and *Jack*
        Janiels until it's
no longer funny and
        tells us all
to bugger off

reliable information

Phil is constantly
    late in the morning
        and constantly
    getting a ticking off
          for talking
on his mobile phone
      and constantly
spilling coffee over
    Alan the endangered himp's desk
      who automatically
lifts his stuff
      out of the way
and continues typing
      without a blink
        and constantly
    standing silently beside me
with his hands in his pockets
      until I look around
so he can tell me
        I'm completely
wasting my life

door crime

as you walk up
    the mile-long ramp
        towards the automatic doors
            you know
              they're going to start closing
agonisingly
    slowly
when you're
  5 metres away
giving you just enough time
      to speed up
   and jam yourself
into the gap
    and force
the doors open
as you pray that
      nobody's watching
           because you'll
      be taken
to Room 101

cloud cuckoo

George the Orwell lookalike
                hovers
at the top floor window
        of our futuristic
early Seventies municipal block
           and stares
                over the roofs
                      of The Town
while sincerely enthusing
Doesn't it remind you
of Constantinople?
                and receiving
                  a short answer
which isn't the one
he was hoping to hear

war correspondent

as the twin towers collapse
  live on tv
and the phones begin to ring
        and we all stand around
imagining the imminent
       end of the world
in our own lonely tower
        only Nostrildamus
remains at his post
    as he tries
       to attach
his report

transporter malfunction

the operator
           puts a call through
to who she thinks
     is the right person
but turns out
   to be entirely
the wrong person
who tries to transfer
           it on
to the right person
         but they aren't there
so someone else answers
               and tries
to transfer it back
   to the switchboard
but proceeds to
balls it up
           completely
and the caller
     is left in p
ie c
    e
     s
in the ether
like someone
out of *Star Trek*

rocket science

Lurch zooms up
in his sensible grey suit
          and I-was-born-for-
information-technology specs
    and puts his mouth
  precisely too close
        to my left ear
and quietly sings
We're All bound
for Mu-Mu Land
     before vanishing
at warp factor 5
into the Gents toilet
        for exactly
fifteen minutes
and twenty seconds

tea time

Prince John
   wonders what
 it would be like
    to be invisible
  and go places
you wouldn't normally
  be able to go
and how you wouldn't
   need to have a bath
and could blame the smell
   on someone else
and
 pretty soon
   we're up to
the speed of light
   and why we'll never
meet extra terrestrials
   because they'll
wipe themselves out
    before they ever get here
and how our Universe is only
  one of
an infinite number
 and why it's best not
to even think about it

fertile ground

the word zips around
   there's a honey
in reception
who's well worth a look
so
  each one has a go
at walking past
      with a file in their hand
and a mask of purpose
          in their stroll
while covertly
eyeing the arse
and licking their lips
and scoring marks out of ten
          until the balance
of blood is restored
        but
God help us
if the men
try the same thing

minority report

Denise the sectarian secretary
        doesn't miss a key
as she enlightens us
     with unrepentant honesty
       that her favourite actor
         is Tom Cruise
     and that
    her favourite chanter
is Frank Sinatra
      and that
        she's got a new job
as a prison warder
      and that
she can't stand papists and pakis
      and that
          the Tsunami is simply
     God's way of keeping
the slant-
     eyed population
down

defective units

Alan the endangered himp
    pretends he's got
           something wrong
          with his brain
and starts
      to do
        a non pc
       spastic walk
along the space
      between
            the ranks of files
as I sing
the Ray Stevens classic
Everything is Beautiful
        and nobody else
            acknowledges
our existence

donkey sanctuary

the pods are chock-a-block
    with bluffers
who will never leave
because they know
    they'll never
        get a job
      anywhere else
  and would be much
better off
    put quietly
       out
of our misery

lost cause

on certain days of the year
  we're told we should
        wear something red
or pink
  or a wacky
        item of clothing
from the least visited part
  of the wardrobe
        as the charity mafia
scour the pods
  and the Huge Head
        tries to prove
he's full of the milk
        of human kindness
as he donates a coin
  into the bucket
        and keeps
his jaw-dropping salary intact

laptop dancer

Bungle the Bear
    hurries in early
      and types her reports
as fast as she can
        and races off to meetings
        and gets all excited
    and types
          as fast as she can
          and types a bit more
          until the keys begin to spin
and goes home as late
        as she can
        and plugs in the laptop
and types everything
        as fast as she can
        and goes to bed
and dreams about typing
      and never allows the terror
    that maybe there's
              nothing else
      that she's got
to take hold

cabin fever

Alan the endangered himp
    who's recently
completely
    given up smoking
stands beside me
in his smoking jacket
which smells
   forever
and quietly says
I like these
comfortable silences
    before
  proceeding
to waggle his tie
    like Oliver Hardy
      and give us
an uncomfortable rendition
of *Perverts in the Night*

bad taste

the Huge Head
      has demanded that
the naughty boy
  who is urinating daily
    on the cubicle floor
should desist immediately
        unless
you're a Chief Officer
        but
there's no mention
  of the anatomically accurate
drawings of male
     and female organs
  on the walls and door
    and vital information
        such as
I'VE GOT A TEN INCHER
     and YOUR MOTHER
          SUCKS COCKS IN HELL
     which
could very well be
here

paper jam

people stand
at the photocopier
         and
            quickly
work themselves towards
spontaneous combustion
         because
the pages stick together in the feeder
or there are smudges across the page
              or
A4 comes out on A3
or the paper runs out
              or
someone has put in purple paper
or the paper mangles up
              or
there is Tipp-Ex on the glass
              or
DNA on the glass
              or
              only
our ridiculous contorted faces
snarling back at us

and relax

Alan the endangered himp
announces it's time
    to get a grip and show
a little *sang-froid*
as he goes through life
  instead of
          always being
     a fizzing ball
of doubt and bitterness
    and regret and anger and
umpteen other words
  that spring to mind
          so we
decide to
  look up *sang-froid*
    in the dictionary
to see what it means
but the page has
     been pulled out
which really
     REALLY
pisses him off

press gang

Sonar Sid the half-mast kid
     hurries to the shredder
then back to his desk
       then hurries to the scanner
then back to his desk
with his too-short
Battle of Trafalgar trousers
          flapping about his ankles
and drops off
in his seat
at lunchtime
      with everyone
slowly turning the pages
   of their broadsheets
and talking very softly
     so as not to wake him up
and taking pictures
    of him on their
mobile phones

block buster

King Man comes up
   and asks me
       who would be who
if all the pod people
      were characters
from *Star Wars*
          and we both agree
     Mini Pip would be
    the Evil Emperor
   and Bungle the Bear
      would be Darth Vader
and Sonar Sid
would be C3PO
   and Alan the endangered himp
        would be Yoda and
everyone else would be
such and such until
eventually I'm the only one left
      so I must be
Jabba the Hutt

unnatural habitat

in summer
it's boiling
         and
in winter it's freezing
             and
when the wind blows
   from the South
  the animal tannery
stench   drifts
         in
through the non-adjustable
sick building ventilation
and everyone takes
it in turn to screw
their face up
    and say
What a honk!
with
    our lives
        infinitely
before us
    and
 the smell of death
in our nostrils

ladies man

John the fount of knowledge
    tells me
   if you stand
    at the right hand urinal
and look over
      your right shoulder
         someone WILL
eventually
open the door of the Gents
at exactly the same time
      someone opens
the door of the Ladies
        on the other side
         of the corridor
   and a lucky woman
will have the thrill
of watching you urinate
      if you
have enough patience
and a big enough bladder

hot desking

when the bell begins
    to banshee non-stop
we know it's time
    to leave our
human belongings behind
       and
    wind
           down
the Lovecraft stairs
and into the usual rain
      to talk to people
we promised never to
        talk to again
as we wait for the sign
      to return to our desks
and recommence
    our relationship with
the coffee or custard
      creams or
    preferably just
remain in our pods and burn

baby food

the young girls
    bring in
their babies
     to show
to the ones
      who have still
  to do it
   and
the ones
     who have done it all
     who
take it in turns
to carry them about
     and pat their backs
and hunger for something
  solid in
their lives
        as
the sound of crying
        fills the office
     and the boys
talk about football

definite article

Prince John tells us
                that he's
definitely going
    to buy a flat
any day now
      and he's found one
which appears
to be turning green
in the middle
of some hellhole
and it's been lying empty
for months
            and the owners are
                in jail
        and is definitely exactly
what he's looking for
        and he definitely hopes
it's probably going
to be okay

resigner bubble

Mick the Stick
doesn't care
that those he's meant
to supervise
        spend half their time
chatting on the phone
  or reading the paper
or discussing *Reality*
    or looking in catalogues
or looking in *Appointments*
        or having 2 hour lunches
or boiling kettle after kettle
        after kettle
       because
he's got a new job
and very soon he'll never see
any of them
        ever
again

recycle bin

at Steven's leaving do
   he lays out the cakes
and says
     he's running
to escape
        this induced narcolepsy
and how he's going to miss
      the ones who
   always remain
     as
he takes his place
       at the turnstile
for ethereal people
     who spin off
into the sunset
     clutching their vouchers
and flowers and *Sorry You're*
   Leaving cards
filled with stuff like
   Take Care and *Good Luck*
and *Keep In Touch*
which they won't

set menu

when someone gets a new job
we plod to a restaurant
                to sit there
saying *well done*
        and smiling
and sipping juice
and eating food
      which reaches
new heights of mediocrity
          and glancing
every few minutes
     at our watches
as we calculate
           the flexi time
that's going to waste

new start

people begin their jobs
    with great expectations
      and fluffy sparkling eyes
        and serious clean suits
and jazzy upbeat ties
           but
    after precisely
        two and a
    half weeks
        you can see
the thousand yard stare
    starting to take over
and the skin turning
    a sunless grey
and the carelessly flung
  anything-will-do clothes
and the sagging shoulders
 and the workhouse expressions
that clearly say
      Dear God
please let me die

bad magnet

at frequent intervals
throughout the day
    Alan the endangered himp
          or Lurch
  or Big Chief Swaldodo
take it in turns
    to stand at my desk
  and talk
about
Squeak or *Ping*
    or any other names
that bat food might be called
  if it was available in the shops
      or sing
the *Stingray* theme tune
    or make twittering noises
or talk about
      how useless
everyone else in the world is
    as Mini Pip marches past
  with a pile of P45s
and looks at us
      triumphantly
over his specs

glass ceiling

a bird
   bigger than
a sparrow
     and smaller
than a starling
       gets trapped
in the Gents toilet
        and doesn't find
the way out
          for a very long time
because
        it keeps on
flying against the closed half
      of the window
then sitting on
      the cubicle door
becoming quietly
    more bewildered
with its beak wide open
   and not even seeing what
is always there in front
of our eyes

inappropriate use

Tony Loony
 Blu-Tacks
two black flippers
and two webbed feet
    onto a big red extinguisher
     which he reckons
looks just like a penguin
  and draws
         two big sad eyes
    onto a cardboard box
   thus creating
Pengy who is good
 and *Box* who isn't
 as they battle
  for possession
of our souls across   the chasm
      of eternity
or something
like that

love story

Alan the endangered himp
   comes in
       and sings
 the latest song
that was playing over
the p.a. system
in the shopping centre
       he walks through
on his way to work
  every morning
which today is
No Woman No Cry
   and yesterday was
Everybody Hurts or *Lyin'*
   Eyes or *If You Leave Me Now* or
      Yesterday or *Me and Mrs Jones*
or *Meet Me On the Corner* or *Have I Told*
   You Lately That I Love
You or *Harvest For the World* as
the words fuse together and
   we plant
a way to survive

vanishing point

we have to wear
    identity cards
on cords
       around our necks
but
    over the years
      the face in the photo
       streaks and blurs
and makes the person
            look like
they're moving
        very fast or
very slowly until one day
we cease
to

log off

      and some
compete for a socket
      and some
don't reply when you say hello
          and some
don't say thank you
when you hold the exit open
          and some
   create a religion
from the necessity of work
          and some
become insane to remain sane
            and some
   pick their nose
when they think no-one's watching
            and some
don't care who's watching
            and some
believe in what they are doing
          and some
don't do what they believe in
         and some
   are in it together
         and some
have been here forever
         and some
have never arrived
       and some
discover true love
  in the corridors
of the least likely
       and some
allow it to roll away
        and some
   look straight into the sun
until there's nothing left to see
          and some

fill their stapler before it runs out
                    and some
put the milk in before
                    and some
put the milk in after
                    and some
prefer it with the light on
                            and some
prefer it with
                the light
out

nostra bamus

King Man comes up
   and tells me that
if mankind ceased to exist
        tomorrow
then all the buildings
would decay
   faster than you think
    the steel
would corrode
   the glass would
fall out
   the paint would
flake off
and only the tyres
of the cars would be left
to prove we were here
      and nature would
reclaim the planet
  and it would
be totally cool
and he really hopes
he's around to see it